بسم الله الرحمن الرحيم

THE ROLE OF *IJTIHĀD* IN LEGISLATION

THE ROLE OF *IJTIHĀD* IN LEGISLATION

Murtaḍā Muṭahharī

Translated by
Mahliqa Qara'i

A catalogue record for this book is available from the British Library and the Australian National Library

Shia Books Australia
www.shiabooks.com.au
info@shiabooks.com.au

ISBN 978-1-922583-39-0

This English edition first published in 2016
Second Edition 2021

Cover picture by @mnshots

Contents

Contents ... V
Transliteration ... VII
Preface ... IX
Biography of the Author ... 1
Introduction ... 7
Ijtihād in the *Sunnī* Tradition ... 11
Ijtihād in the *Shīʿah* Tradition ... 31
Akhbārism in the Imāmiyyah Tradition ... 43
Bibliography ... 59
Index ... 61

Transliteration

Symbol	Transliteration	Symbol	Transliteration
ء	'	أ	a
ب	b	ت	t
ث	th	ج	j
ح	ḥ	خ	kh
د	d	ذ	dh
ر	r	ز	z
س	s	ش	sh
ص	ṣ	ض	ḍ
ط	ṭ	ظ	ẓ
ع	'	غ	gh
ف	f	ق	q
ک	k	ل	l
م	m	ن	n
ه	h	و	w
ی	y	ة	ah
Long Vowels		Short Vowels	
آ	a	ـَ	a
ای	ī	ـِ	i
او	ū	ـُ	u
Persian Letters			
Symbol	Transliteration	Symbol	Transliteration
پ	p	چ	ch
ژ	zh	گ	g

At the end of Farsi words, 'eh', '-e', and '-ye' have been used.

Preface

Considering necessity of preparing appropriate Islamic texts in English for the modern world and aiming at satisfying that need, Al-Mustafa International Research Institute (M.I.R.I.) was established in 2009. This centre has accomplished that duty in the best way by producing, translating, and reprinting tens of such appropriate texts. The present book entitled *The Role of ijtihād in Legislation* is among them.

The Role of ijtihād in Legislation is originally a lecture delivered by the great Muslim thinker and reformer Āyatullāh Murtaḍā Muṭahharī after the death of Āyatullāh Burūjirdī in 1962, in which he surveys and expounds the concept of *ijtihād* and its characteristics.

This booklet deals with such topics as the

meaning of *ijtihād*, its root in the *sunnī* and the *shī'ah* traditions and appearance of Akhbārism in Islamic society.

The English translation of this book was published many years ago by Al-Tawḥīd journal (Vol.4, N.2). Now, Islam and West Research Center (I.W.R.C.) has the honor to present this book to the dear readers in a new form. In the present edition the biography of the author, transliteration of expressions as well as Farsi and Arabic names, bibliography and index are added by Al-Mustafa International Research Institute (M.I.R.I.) in order to make the book more precise and beneficial.

We hope that this book will be an invaluable contribution to the Islamic thought and be of value for both lay readers and men of research.

We take this opportunity to express our gratitude to "Islam and West Research Centre Ltd" for publishing this book and hope that the latter should form a link showing the way for those who seek advancement.

Al-Mustafa International Research Institute (M.I.R.I.)

Biography of the Author

Murtaḍā Muṭahharī was born in a village some forty kilometres from Mashhad in 1338/1919–20. He received his earliest education mostly at the hands of his father and while still a child entered the *Ḥawza 'Ilmiyya*, the traditional educational establishment, of Mashhad, but soon afterwards left for Qum, the centre for religious education in Iran. While he was pursuing elementary studies there he was greatly affected by the lessons in *akhlāq* (Islamic ethics) given by Āyatullāh Imām Khumaynī, which Muṭahharī himself described as being, in reality, lessons in *ma'ārif wa sayr u-sulūk* (the theoretical and practical approaches to mysticism). He later studied metaphysics (*falsafa*) with him, as well as jurisprudence (*uṣūl al-fiqh*). He was especially attracted by *falsafa*, theoretical mysticism (*'irfān*) and theology (*Kalām*), known as 'intellectual knowledge', and he went on to study these subjects with 'Allāma Ṭabāṭabā'ī. His teachers in law (*fiqh*) were all important figures of the time, especially Āyatullāh Burūjirdī, who became the authoritative jurisconsult (*marja'-e taqlīd*), as well as head of the *Ḥawza 'Ilmiyya* of Qum, in 1945. Murtaḍā Muṭahharī studied both *fiqh* and *uṣūl al-fiqh* in the classes of Āyatullāh Burūjirdī for ten years. He was also deeply affected at about this time by lessons on *Nahj al-Balāghah* given by Mīrzā 'Alī Āqā Shīrāzī Iṣfahānī, whom he had met in Isfahan. He later said that, although he had been reading this work since his childhood, he now felt that he had discovered a 'new world'. Subsequently, Muṭahharī became a well-known teacher in Qum, first in Arabic language and literature, and later in logic (*Manṭiq*), *uṣūl al-fiqh*, *falsafa* and mysticism.

In 1952 Murtaḍā Muṭahharī moved to Tehran, where, two years later, he began teaching in the Theology Faculty of the University. Not only did he make a strong impression on students, but his move to Tehran also meant that he could become involved with organizations for political and social change. These Islamic associations were groups of students, engineers, doctors, merchants, etc., set up during the 1950s and 1960s; they formed the nucleus of the movement that was eventually to become the revolution. He was also a founder member of the Ḥusainiyya Irshād, which played a central role in the religious life of the capital during the four years of its existence until its closure by the authorities in 1973. At the same time he maintained his contact with traditional religious activities, teaching first in the Madrasa Marwī in Tehran and later back in Qum, and also preaching in mosques in Tehran and elsewhere in the country. Through his lectures, articles and books he became a famous and much-respected figure throughout Iran, but it was mainly among the students and teachers of the schools and universities that he was most influential, setting an example and inspiring them as a committed and socially aware Muslim with a traditional education who could make an intellectually appropriate and exciting response to modern secularizing tendencies.

His wide-ranging knowledge and scholarship are reflected in the scope of his writings, which cover the fields of law, philosophy, theology, history and literature. He was also one of the few high-ranking *'ulamā* to be in continuous contact with Imām Khumaynī during the fifteen or so years in which the movement that led to the revolution was developing. He was actively engaged in all the stages of this movement. His life came to an abrupt and untimely end when he was shot in the street by an assassin after a meeting of the Revolutionary Council on the evening of 1 May 1979. Many mourners accompanied his funeral cortege from Tehran to Qum, where he was buried near the shrine of the sister of the eighth *Shī'ī* Imām. Shahīd Muṭahharī contributed a great deal to Islamic scholarship through his many publications, most of which have been translated into English. They include: *Training and Education in Islam*(Amin Research and Cultural Centre,Kuala Lumpur,2011), *The theory of knowledge: An Islamic Perspective*(Amin Research and Cultural Centre,Kuala Lumpur,2011),*Islamic Modest Dress* (Macmillan Publishing Company, Inc., 1990); *Universal Prototype*, translated by Laleh Bakhtiar (Abjad Book Designers & Builders, 1989); *Ḥijāb*, translated by Laleh Bakhtiar (Abjad Book Designers & Builders, 1993); *Iqbāl* (Abjad Book Designers & Builders, 1993); *Reviving Islamic Ethos*; *Master and Mastership*; *Jurisprudence and Its Principles*; *Spiritual Discourses*; *The Awaited Saviour*; *Light within Me*; *The Goal of Life*; Man and Universe; *Polarization Around the Character of 'Alī Ibn Abī Ṭālib*; *Woman and Her Rights*; and *Anecdotes of Pious Men*.

Apart from the above-mentioned books, there are many other published works in Arabic and Persian.

Introduction

The terms '*mujtahid*' and '*ijtihād*' are nowadays among those which have acquired great currency, even sanctity, among the *shī'ah*. One would be surprised to know that the term *ijtihād* was formerly, from the times of the Prophet (S) and for several successive centuries, a Sunnī term. It became Shia after undergoing a change of meaning, or what would be more precise to say, the term remained specifically Sunnī for several centuries and became 'Muslim', in the wider sense, that is, after undergoing a change of meaning and dissociating itself from its earlier particular sense.

As to its not being a *shī'ah* term formerly, there is no doubt; if there is any uncertainty, it is about the date of its acceptance by the *shī'ah.* It is not improbable that this term like several groups of people in the seventh century was converted to Shī'ism at the hands of the absolute Āyatullāh, al-'Allāmah al-Ḥillī. However, as we shall presently explain, the conversion came after its undergoing a change of meaning.

Apparently, there seems to be no doubt that this term was never used by any of the Imāms of the Ahl al-Bayt (A.S.). The terms *ijtihād* and *mujtahid*, in the sense in which they are used by *shī'ah* and *sunnī fuqahā'*, have not been used in any of their *aḥādīth.* Neither they themselves were ever known by the epithet '*mujtahid*' nor did they ever use it for the scholars and legists from among their companions. Otherwise the root relating to such terms as *fatwā* and *iftā'*, which convey approximately the modern sense of *ijtihād*, and its derivatives do occur in the *aḥādīth.* For instance, al-Imām al-Bāqir (A.S.) is reported to have said to Abān Ibn Taghlib:

> Sit in the mosque of al-Madinah and give *fatwās* for the people. Indeed I love more like you to be seen amongst my *shīʿah.*[1]

And in a famous *ḥadīth*, al-Imām al-Ṣādiq (A.S.) is reported to have said to ʿUnwān al-Baṣrī:

> Avoid giving *fatwā* in the way you would run away from a lion; do not make your neck a bridge for the people.

The reason for the former unpopularity of the word is that during the early centuries of the Islamic era - that is also the period in which the Imāms of the Ahl al-Bayt (A.S.) lived - the word, due to the specific meaning it carried, was not acceptable to the Imāms (A.S.). Naturally, it could not have played any role in their teachings. However, after undergoing a gradual change of meaning, when it came to be used in a different sense by *sunnī fuqahā'* themselves, it

1. Ḥussain Nūrī al-Ṭabrisī, *Mustadrak al-Wasā'il wa Mustanbaṭ al-Masā'il*, vol.17,315.

was also adopted by *shīʿīte fiqh.* Now we shall briefly describe the background of the *sunnī* usage of this term.

Ijtihād in the *Sunnī* Tradition

Sunnī scholars narrate a *ḥadīth* that the Prophet (S), while sending Mu'ādh to Yemen, asked him as to on what he would base his judgment. "In accordance with the Book of Allah", replied Mu'ādh, "*But what if you don't find it there?*" inquired the Prophet (S). "According to the Sunnah of the Apostle of Allah", replied Mu'ādh. "*But what if you don't find it there too?*" asked the Prophet (S) again. 'I will exert my own opinion', replied Mu'ādh. The Prophet (S) put his hand on Mu'ādh's chest and said: "*Thank God for assisting His Apostle with what he loves.*" [1]

They have narrated other traditions on the

---

1. Aḥmad Ḥanbal, *Musnad*, vol.36, 333, no.22007

subject to the effect that either the Prophet (S) directly commanded his Companions to exercise *ijtihād* in case they could not find a rule in the Book and the Sunnah, or to the effect that he approved of the practice of his Companions that practiced *ijtihād*. To the *sunnīs*, this is something definite, confirmed by consensus (*ijmā'*).

About the Holy Prophet (S) himself, they have said that some of his injunctions were purely based on personal *ijtihād* not on revelation. Even in their works on jurisprudence (*'ilm al-uṣūl*) the problem is raised whether or not the Prophet (S) could make errors in his personal *ijtihād*. They have narrated traditions in this regard and transmitted reports of the Companions as to how they justified their own actions or those of others on the basis of *ijtihād*. We abstain from quoting any of them here for the sake of brevity.

It is evident that in all the above instances the term *ijtihād* is not used in its current sense, that is, making the utmost effort in deducing rules of the *Sharīʿah* from the related sources (*adillah*). The meaning of *ijtihād* there is 'exercising of one's opinion or judgement' (*al-ʿamal bi al-ra'y*). It means that in a case where the Divine dicta are absent or implicit, one should see what would be more acceptable to one's intelligence and taste, or nearer to truth and justice, or analogous to other Islamic laws, and to adopt it for his judgement.

Accordingly, *ijtihād* is also accounted as one of the sources of Islamic legislation, like the *Qur'an* and the Sunnah, although not as a source parallel to these two. So long as a rule is to be found in the *Qur'an* and the Sunnah, the need for *ijtihād* does not arise. However, in absence of relevant dicta in the *Qur'an*, the Sunnah or *ijmāʿ*, *ijtihād* becomes a source of legislation. On this basis, they have said that the sources of legislation are four: the Book, the Sunnah, *ijmāʿ*, and *ijtihād* (i.e. *qiyās*).

Also, according to this approach, *ijtihād* is not synonymous with expertise in Islamic law (*faqāhah*), nor is the term *mujtahid* synonymous with *faqīh*. Rather, *ijtihād* is one of the functions of the *faqīh*. The *faqīh* should have knowledge of the *Qur'an* and the *ḥadīth* corpus; he should be able to distinguish the *nāsikh* from the *mansūkh*, the *'āmm* from the *khāṣṣ*, the *mujmal* from the *mubayyan*,and the *muḥkam* from the *mutashābih*.

He should be familiar with the Qur'anic vocabulary and terminology, know the circumstances in which a particular verse was revealed (*sha'n al-nuzūl*), and have knowledge of the successive generations of narrators and transmitters of *ḥadīth*. He should also be able to reconcile the apparently conflicting traditions. In addition to all that, he should practice *ijtihād* and exercise his personal judgements in particular cases.

What was the character and basis of that *itihād*? Did the term *ijtihād* found in *ḥadīth* mean exercising *qiyās*? Did the Prophet (S) and his Companions practice *ijtihād* in this sense. Did it also apply to other practices such as *istiḥsān*? Al-Shāfi'ī, in his famous *Risālah*, has a chapter on *ijtihād*, which follows the one on *ijmā'*, and is itself followed by one on *istiḥsān*. In his discussion of the subject, al-Shāfi'ī draws the conclusion that the *ijtihād* prescribed by the *Sharī'ah* is confined to *qiyās* and that other types of *ijtihād*, such as *istiḥsān*, do not have any canonical grounds. Al-Shāfi'ī believes that the canonical grounds for *qiyās* are identical with those for *ijtihād*.

There were other questions that were debated by *sunnī fuqahā'*, such as: Are *ijtihād* and *al-'amal bi al-ra'y* confined to cases where there is no express text (*naṣṣ*) or whether one may do *ijtihād* (called *ta'awwul* in this case) and exercise his judgement despite the presence of express texts? What are the conditions applicable to Sunnah if it is to preponderate *ijtihād*? Are all traditions narrated from the Prophet (S) to be relied upon and given precedence over *ijtihād*? Is reliable *ḥadīth* confined to those which are *mashhūr* and *mustafīḍ*, as Abū Ḥanīfah believed? Who are those who had the right of *ijtihād* and whose *ijtihād* was binding (*ḥujjah*) for the others? On what grounds have the others no right to go against their *ijtihād*? Evidently, to go into the details of each of these questions is outside the scope of this paper. However, it is necessary to mention some relevant points here:

1. The position of the *fuqahā'* and Imāms of the Ahl al-Sunnah with respect to the acceptability of *ijtihād*, in the above-mentioned sense, is not the same. Some of them give a wider scope to *ijtihād* and *qiyās* and some restrict it. Some altogether reject *qiyās* and *ijtihād.*

Abū Ḥanīfah, who lived in Iraq and was considered the jurist of the 'Irāqīs, because of the many conditions he required for a tradition to be acceptable, and also on account of being distant from the centre of *ḥadīth*, which was the Ḥijāz, had lesser knowledge of *ḥadīth.* Also due to other reasons, including his background of *kalām* and logic, he took greater recourse to *qiyās* and on this account was strongly opposed by the *sunnī* jurists of his time and those who came after him.

Mālik Ibn Anas spent his life in al-Madinah and made lesser use of *qiyās*. Reportedly, he did not use *qiyās* except in a few cases, and, according to a report of Ibn Khallekān, was greatly repentant at the time of his death of having taken recourse to *qiyās* in his *fatwās* even in those few cases.

Al-Shāfi'ī, who belonged to the 'Irāqī school and had studied under Abū Ḥanīfah's pupils and had as well studied under Mālik in al-Madinah, took a middle road between Mālik and Abū Ḥanīfah.

Aḥmad Ibn Ḥanbal was more a *muḥaddith* than a *faqīh* and avoided *qiyās* even to a greater extent than Mālik Ibn Anas.

Dāwūd Ibn 'Alī al-Ẓāhirī al-Iṣfahānī, the founder of the Ẓāhirī school, was altogether opposed to the practice of *qiyās* and regarded it as an innovation (*bid'ah*) in the faith.

As a consequence of these differences there emerged among the Ahl al-Sunnah two general trends: one of them was represented by the Ahl al-Ḥadīth and the other by the Ahl al-Ra'y. The Ahl al-Ḥadīth, or the Traditionists, attached lesser or no significance to *qiyās* and *ra'y* and the Ahl al- Ra'y in turn relied to a lesser extent on *aḥādīth*.

2. Concurrently with the emergence of the Ahl al- Ra'y and the Ahl al-Ḥadīth, a problem that arose among the contemporary circles of *kalām* was that of the rational basis of legal judgements (*al-ḥusn wa al-qubḥ al-'aqliyyah*). Although at first sight there seems to be no link between these two developments, because one of them belonged to *fiqh* and took place in juristic circles and the other belonged to the circles of *kalām*, but, as pointed by some historians, the theory of rational basis of judgement - which was raised by the Mu'tazilah and who staunchly defended it - was also intended to find some kind of basis for *ijtihād*, i.e. *qiyās* and the practice of *ra'y*.

According to this theory, the laws of the *Sharī'ah* were based on a series of real benefits and harms and that human reason was capable of independently discovering those benefits and harms inherent in things; therefore reason was capable of discovering the purposes and criteria of the laws of religion through *ijtihād* and *ra'y*.

This conjecture is further strengthened if we remember that the Ahl al-Ḥadīth, who later, in the fourth/tenth century, came to be known as Ashā'irah, represented the chief opposition to the Mu'tazilah.

3. Right from the first century, from the time when groups of people gathered in mosques for the purpose of study and debate, some persons debated about the issues of *ḥalāl* and *ḥarām*. They gathered around them pupils and adherents from among the common people, who regarded their *fatwās* as authoritative and referred to them their questions about *ḥalāl* and *ḥarām*.

Such was the beginning of the gradual development of a class of scholars who later came to be called *fuqahā'* . Every region, city and group followed a certain individual, and the rulers had not yet adopted the policy of following the *fatwās* of a certain jurist as official law.

The emergence of this class of jurists did not require any special conditions. Occasionally, social conditions demanded that one prominent individual should be recognized by the people and followed in religious precepts. Gradually, this resulted in the emergence of diverse legal approaches and schools, which in turn were preserved and perpetuated by the pupils of the originator after his death. In this way, various legal schools and sects emerged amongst the *sunnīs*, the most famous of them being the Ḥanafī, the Shāfi'ī, the Mālikī, the Ḥanbalī and the Ẓāhirī schools.

Of course, the founders of these schools were not the only early jurists and *mujtahidūn* that were there. There were others who held their own legal opinions and were not followers of anyone. However, this independence gradually disappeared after the fourth/tenth century and no independent *mujtahid* emerged after this time in the *Sunnī* tradition.

Apparently, the last person to have been an independent *mujtahid* with his own independent approach in legal issues was the well-known historian and exegete Muḥammad Ibn Jarīr al-Ṭabarī (d. 310/922), who although famous for his work on history, is considered a *sunnī faqīh* of the first rank.

The later *sunnī mujtahids* were either *al-mujtahid al-muṭlaq al-muntasib* or *mujtahid al-fatwā*(also occasionally known as *mujtahid al-madhhab*). '*Al-mujtahid al-muṭlaq al-muntasib*' means a *mujtahid* who is attached to one of the well-known schools and follows the juristic approach of its founder but in deducing legal rules, on the basis of the school's juristic principles, he may formulate his own independent legal opinions which may be different from the legal opinions of the founder.

For instance, while being a Shāfi'ī or a Ḥanafī in jurisprudence, he may differ with al-Shāfi'īs or Abū Ḥanīfah's express *fatwās* in legal matters. A number of eminent *sunnī* jurists are considered to belong to this class, such as: Imām al-Ḥaramayn al-Juwaynī, Abū Ḥāmid Muḥammad al-Ghazālī, Ibn al-Ṣabbāgh, and others.

'*Mujtahid al-madhhab*' or '*mujtahid al-fatwā*' is someone who follows the founder of the school in all matters in which the founder has expressly given his views. However in issues in which he does find an opinion of the founder, he may exercise his own *ijtihād* and give *fatwā*.

Accordingly, *ijtihād* is of three kinds: independent *ijtihād*, semi-independent *ijtihād* (*al-ijtihād al-muṭlaq al-muntasib*), and *ijtihād* within the framework of the juristic and legal positions of a school (*ijtihād al-fatwā*).

In any case, the *mujtahids* who came after the fourth century did not find any followers. On the other hand the *mujtahids* who came before this period were not limited to the four Imāms of the popular schools; there were nine other eminent jurists of whom some lived before the four Imāms - such as al-Ḥasan al-Baṣrī - some were their contemporaries - such as Sufyān al-Thawrī - and some who came after them - such as Dāwūd al-Ẓāhirī and Muḥammad Ibn Jarīr al-Ṭabarī - and all of them had more or less followers among the people.

However, there was a gradual rise in the followers of the four Imāms, for, according to al-Miqfrīzī in *al-Khiṭaṭ*, al-Malik al-Ẓāhir, the ruler of Egypt, officially declared in the year 665/1257 that except the four schools - Shāfi'ī ,Mālikī, Ḥanafī and Ḥanbalī - other schools had no official recognition and that no judge had the right to give judgement except on the basis of the four schools. The people were also strictly forbidden to follow any except the four schools. This was the beginning of the restriction of the official schools to four.'

This brief description shows that when we talk of the closure of the door of *ijtihād* in the *sunnī* tradition, we refer to the *ijtihād* of the first kind, i.e. independent *ijtihād*. As to the second kind (*al-ijtihād al-muṭlaq al-muntasib*) and the third kind (*ijtihād al-madhhab*), their doors have remained open.

Why should the doors of independent *ijtihād* have been closed after the fourth century and no one should have right to complete independence and be bound to follow one of the Imāms in jurisprudence? Why and for what reason is it not permissible today to follow anyone except the four Imāms?

Why should one who follows any one of the Imāms follow him in all issues and have no right to follow the other three by exercising discretion in some issues? *sunnī* scholars have given various answers to all of these questions and none of them is convincing.

Shāh Walī Allah Dihlawī (d. 1180/1765), in a treatise (*risālah*) called *"al-Inṣāf fī Bayān Sabab al-Ikhtilāf"* - which has been quoted by Farīd al-Wajdī under *jahada* in the *Dā'irat al-Ma'ārif*, with the remark that it is the best treatise written on the topic - acclaims the closure of the door of independent *ijtihād* and the latter scholars' imitation of one of the early Imāms and says:

that is, 'It is a secret that God Almighty has inspired in the scholars with' to safeguard Islam and protect the religion from disintegration. Farīd al-Wajdī himself does not approve of the prohibition on *ijtihād* and does not confirm those words of Shāh Walī Allah.

Two years ago, according to what we have read in papers and have heard, the great 'Allāmah Shaykh Maḥmūd Shaltūt, the *muftī* and rector of al-Azhar University, with great courage characteristic of great reformers, broke this thousand-year-old spell and officially announced that the door of *ijtihād* is open and that there is nothing objectionable about a follower of one school referring to the judgements of another school in case they are supported by firmer arguments.

He also announced in an official *fatwā* that it is correct to follow the Ja'farī school of *fiqh*, just like the other schools. Subsequently, a chair of comparative legal studies was established at al-Azhar. Undoubtedly this was the greatest step that was taken since the beginnings of Islamic jurisprudence for the sake of the benefit and general welfare of Muslims. Its worth will be better recognized in the future.

4. Another problem related to the subject of *ijtihād* is that of *takhṭi'ah* (admission of the possibility of error in the judgements of the *mujtahid*) and *taṣwīb* (confirmation of the *mujtahid*'s infallibility and denial of any possibility of error), which has throughout been a topic of debate in books on *kalām* and *uṣūl al-fiqh*. Generally, it is mentioned in books on *uṣūl* that the *shī'ah fuqahā'* admit possibility of error in the *mujtahid*'s *fatwās* and are accordingly called *mukhaṭṭi'ah* (derived from *khata'*: error), whereas the *sunnī fuqahā'* believe that the *mujtahid* is always right in his judgements, and are hence called *muṣawwibah* (derived from *ṣawāb*: that which is right).

However, it is not the case that all the *sunnī fuqahā'* support *taṣwīb*; rather, only a small number of them have accepted this view. In any case, for the *shī'ah*, who define *ijtihād* as 'the effort to deduce the real law from the sources of the *Sharīʿah*', it is difficult to imagine that every *mujtahid* should be always right.

It is not possible that whatever any *mujtahid* may judge should be correct and his judgement should be the real law; for it is possible that different *mujtahids* may hold divergent opinions simultaneously about a certain subject and the same *mujtahid* may hold different opinions at different times about the same issue. How is it possible that he should always be right?

The roots of the theory of *taṣwīb* lie in a certain theory of *ijtihād* which is held by those who define *ijtihād* as the practice of *qiyās* and ra'y . They claim that the laws received by the Prophet (S) through revelation are limited, whereas issues and problems which require legislation are unlimited in number. Therefore, the laws given by the Divine Lawgiver are not adequate to meet the requirements.

Accordingly, God has given the right to the scholars of the Ummah, or a group of them, to employ their personal taste and intelligence in cases where there are no religious dicta and select something which resembles other Islamic laws and is closer to the criteria of justice and truth. In accordance with this reasoning, they accept the theory of *taṣwīb*, for, according to this view of *ijtihād*, it is itself one of the sources of the Divine Law.

The idea of *taṣwīb* was unimaginable to the minds of *shīʿah* jurisprudent, because they had taken for granted the principle that every event or problem should have a real Divine law related to it. *Ijtihād*, to them, meant inquiry and effort to discover that law with the help of reliable canonical sources. Of course, in the light of such an outlook of *ijtihād* it is impossible that every *mujtahid* should be right.

The theory of *taṣwīb*, however, does not rest on such an outlook of *ijtihād*. It rests on an outlook which regards it as impossible that God should have legislated laws regarding every kind of situation.

Because, if such were the case, they should have been set forth in the Book and the

Sunnah; but the laws given in the Book and the Sunnah are limited in number, whereas situations are innumerable and unlimited. Hence God has given the *'ulamā* of the Ummah the right to legislate through *ijtihād* such laws as have not been given through revelation. Since this right is God-given, the judgements of the *mujtahid* are the actual laws of God.

The problem of *taṣwīb* and *takhṭi'ah* has been debated a lot in books on *kalām* and *uṣūl*, and here our purpose was just to refer to the above mentioned point. The above discussion related to the *sunnī* background of the term *ijtihād*; now we shall turn to the change of meaning that this term underwent, which resulted in its acceptance by the *shī'ah*.

Ijtihād in the *Shī'ah* Tradition

Until the fourth/tenth and the fifth/eleventh centuries we observe that whenever the word is used by a scholar it carries the sense of *qiyās* and *ra'y*. For instance, Shaykh Abū Ja'far al-Ṭūsī (d. 460/1067), in his *'Uddat al-Uṣūl*, devotes a chapter to *qiyās*. He devotes another chapter to *ijtihād* where he discusses one of the issues related to *ijtihād*, i.e. the problem of *taṣwīb* and *takhṭi'ah*. The book has another chapter entitled "Did the Prophet practice *ijtihād*, and whether it was legitimate for him to practice it? Was it legitimate for the Companions of the Prophet to practice *ijtihād* when they were away from him or were in his presence?" Later, in the course of his discussion, he says: "This controversy is basically uncalled for according to our doctrines, because, as we have proved earlier, *qiyās* and *ijtihād* are absolutely impermissible in the *Sharīʿah.*"

This remark of al-Shaykh al-Ṭūsī shows that until his age the word *ijtihād* was still used in the sense of ra'y and *qiyās*.

Ijtihād lexically means 'putting in utmost effort' in doing something. In the earliest days, the term in accordance with the traditions ascribed to the Prophet (S) and the Companions, was taken to mean *ijtihād bi al-ra'y*, or putting in utmost effort in the exercise of *ra'y* and *qiyās*. However, gradually it took a wider meaning and came to mean putting in utmost effort in discovering the laws of the *Sharīʿah* from its reliable sources. Thus we see that al-Ghazālī (d. 505/1 111) in his *al-Mustaṣfā* - although he uses the word recurringly in its earlier sense of *qiyās*, for instance, when he says:

> They have differed as to the permissibility

> of practicing *qiyās* and *ijtihād* during the days of the Prophet ... [1]

He also uses it in the general sense of scholarly effort on the part of a *faqīh.*

> It (*ijtihād*) means putting in of the utmost effort in doing something. But the term has come to be used in the terminology of scholars specifically for the *mujtahids* putting in of the utmost effort in acquiring the knowledge of the laws of the *Sharīʿah.*[2]

From this time onwards we see that the term is used less frequently in the special sense of *ra'y* and *qiyās* and takes on the sense of scholarly effort in discovering the laws of the *Sharīʿah.* With this change, the term found way into the *shīʿīte fiqh* also, for earlier the *shīʿah* had opposed it on account of their opposition to *ijtihād bi al-ra'y*, not because they were opposed to scholarly diligence.

---

1 . vol. 2, 354.

2 . vol. 2, 350.

In any case, they did not resist its use after it changed its meaning. Probably the first to use this term among the *shīʿah* Imāmiyyah scholars was al-ʿAllāmah al-Ḥillī (d. 726/1326), who accepting it used it in its second sense in his work *Tahdhīb al-Uṣūl*. In that work he devotes a chapter to *ijtihād* and uses it in the sense current today. It seems that it was from this time that the *shīʿah* accepted the word or the word embraced Shīʿīsm.

We said earlier that the opposition to *qiyās* was not limited to the *shīʿah* and there were schools among *sunnīs* who either altogether rejected it and regarded it as a heresy or avoided it as much as possible. The Muʿtazilah, who advanced the doctrine of *al-ḥusn wa al-qubḥ al-ʿaqliyyah*, backed *qiyās* and *ra'y* in their fight against the Ahl al-Ḥadīth who rejected it.

The Ahl al-Ḥadīth, who later came to be called

Ashā'irah due to their approach in *kalām*, rejected the doctrine of *al-ḥusn wa al-qubḥ al-'aqliyyah*, claiming that the desirability or undesirability of things is derived from the commands and prohibitions of the lawgiver and not vice versa. As a result, they denied reason any role in legislation of Divine laws. The controversies between the Mu'tazilah and supporters of *qiyās* and *ra'y* on one side and the Ashā'irah and the Ahl al-Ḥadīth on the other side revolve around the role of reason and its share in legislation.

It must not be concluded from the above discussion that the *shī'ah* opposition to *ra'y* and *qiyās* was also based on the same reasons as those of the Ashā'irah and the Ahl al-Ḥadīth, which was outright opposition to the role of reason in deduction of the laws of the *Sharī'ah*. The Shī'ī opposition to *qiyās* and *ra'y* had two reasons.

The first was that the claim of the supporters of *qiyās* that the Book and the Sunnah are not adequate sources of legislation was not acceptable to the Imāms of the Ahl al-Bayt (A.S.).

In the sermons of the *Nahj al-Balāghah* and other Shī'ī compilations of *ḥadīth* the idea that the Book and the Sunnah are not adequate has been vehemently rejected. In the *Uṣūl al-Kāfī*, the chapter followed by another entitled:

The chapter about referring to the Book and the Sunnah, and that verily there is no *ḥarām* or *ḥalāl* and nothing needed by the people that is not present in the Book or the Sunnah.

The second reason advanced by the *shī'ah* against *qiyās* was that it was based on conjecture and led very frequently to error. These two reasons clearly stand out in the books of early *shī'ah* scholars, and we shall abstain from further details for brevity's sake.

The best evidence of the fact that the *shī'ah* opposition to *qiyās* and *ra'y* was not based on a hostility to the role of reason in canonical matters is that, from the very beginning that the *shī'ah* jurisprudence was committed to writing, reason was considered one of the sources (*adillah*) of law. The *shī'ah* jurisprudent stated that the sources of the *Sharīʿah* are four: the Book, the Sunnah, *ijmāʿ* and *ʿaql* (reason), whereas the Ẓāhirīs and the Ahl al-Ḥadīth confined the *adillah* to the Book, the Sunnah and *ijmāʿ*, and the supporters of *raʾy* and *qiyās* regarded them as four: the Book, the Sunnah, *ijmāʿ* and *qiyās*.

The *shīʿah* jurisprudent, while opposing *qiyās* and *raʾy*, accepted the Muʿtazilah viewpoint about the rational basis of ethico-legal judgements, defended it and did not oppose it like the Ashāʿirah and the Ahl al-Ḥadīth. The concurrence of views between the *shīʿah* and the Muʿtazilah regarding this doctrine and its corollaries - such as the doctrine of Divine justice - led the *shīʿah* among the Muʿtazilah to be known as ʿAdliyyah and the *shīʿah* left behind the Muʿtazilah in their support of the doctrine of Divine justice. As a result, it came to be said in scholarly circles that: "justice and *tawḥīd* are ʿAlawīd and fatalism and anthropomorphism are Umayyad."

The reason for calling justice ʿAlawīd was that the supporters of the Ahl al-Bayt (A.S.) were also defenders of the doctrine of *al-ḥusn wa al-qubḥ al-'aqliyyah* and the doctrine of justice was a corollary to it. As to *tawḥīd* being 'Alawīd, it was on account of the belief in the unity of Divine Essence and Attributes.

The Umayyads supported *jabr* (fatalism) and *tashbīh* (anthropomorphism) due to political exigencies. The issue of the independent capacity of reason to perceive the good and evil of things, and the subsidiary doctrine of justice, became so much a characteristic of the *shī'ah* that justice came to be recognized as one of the principal tenets of the *shī'īte* creed.

That the *shī'īte* opposition to *ra'y* and *qiyās* is not to be taken to have been an opposition to the role of reason in *ijtihād* becomes completely obvious when we examine the extant documentary evidence. At the present the *shī'ah* state the principle of the interrelation of Divine laws and actual benefits and harms and the principle of harmony between reason and religious law in these words:

Whatever is the judgement of reason, is also the judgement of the *Sharī'ah.*

This is an incontrovertible axiom of *shī'īte* jurisprudence. The above discussion makes it clear that the *shī'ah* Imāmiyyah approach to *ijtihād* was an independent one: it was neither bound to *ra'y* and *qiyās*, nor did it impose any bounds on reason in the manner of the Ahl al-Ḥadīth.

The Imāmiyyah jurists on the one hand recognized the rights of reason and regarded it as one of the sources of law, on the other hand they rejected *qiyās* and *ijtihād bi al-ra'y* in their books on jurisprudence, in chapters devoted to *qiyās*. However, it would have been in order if the latter scholars had followed the ancient ones in discussing *qiyās* and *ra'y* in their works.

It would have helped to define the exact limits of the prohibited form of *qiyās*, which would have been better understood. This would have prevented some individuals from waging a battle against reason under the pretext of opposition to *qiyās*.

In fact it would have been better for scholars to devote a separate chapter to reason and rational grounds in their works on jurisprudence, in which they could delineate more precisely the role of reason and also discuss, secondarily, the inadmissibility of *qiyās*. In view of this author, the absence of any discussion by the latter scholars about the inadmissible form of *qiyās* and the limits of the role of reason in legislation has been more or less detrimental to *shī'ah fiqh* and *ijtihād*.

We should know that the great secret of Islam, from the viewpoint of the Imāms of the Ahl al-Bayt (A.S.) , is the principle that the general laws of the Book and the Sunnah are sufficient for satisfying the religious needs of Muslims for all time, and that they have no need of *ra'y* and *qiyās*. It is characteristic of all Islamic laws that they are not only not hindersome to human progress in any era, but are conducive to it by guiding and directing it in the right direction.

All that is needed to grasp this great secret is to have an enlightened and firm grasp of the vital issues. This great secret of the resourcefulness of Islam can also be called 'the great secret of '*ijtihād*'. To be certain, if an independent chapter were devoted to the above topic in books on jurisprudence, some of the existing contradictions and constraints in the relationship between *fiqh* and progress would have been eliminated. This problem requires an independent study and here we shall abstain from going into further details.

In the course of history, those *sunnī* schools of *fiqh* which were more rigid and formalistic and allowed lesser role to reason in deduction of laws, either disappeared gradually or the number of their followers diminished. The Ẓāhirīs, who followed Dāwūd Ibn 'Alī, became altogether extinct. The Ḥanbalī school, which after the Ẓāhirī is the most rigid and formalistic of *sunnī* schools, gradually lost followers, and had it not been for the appearance of Ibn

Taymiyyah, who provided the material on which Wahhābism was later to thrive, perhaps today the number of followers of the Ḥanbalī school would have been very small.

The school of Mālik spread only in North Africa and Maghrib, away from the centers of Islamic culture, and, as Ibn Khaldūn says, the cause of the spreading of the school of Mālik in North Africa and Maghrib was that the inhabitants were Bedouins who lived away from the centers of science and culture. In any case, the rigid and formalistic *sunnī* schools declined and lost followers with the passage of time.

Akhbārism in the Imāmiyyah Tradition

One of the most surprising as well as regrettable phenomena was the emergence of Akhbārism among the *shīʿah* in the early eleventh/seventeenth century. Akhbārism was a hundred times more rigid and formalistic than either the Ẓāhirī or the Ḥanbalī school. Its emergence must be considered a great catastrophe in the *shīʿah* world whose effects more or less survive to the present day, causing stagnation and obscurantism in the *shīʿah* Muslim society.

The founder of Akhbārism was Mullā Amīn Astarābādī, who expounded his beliefs in his famous book *Fawāʾid al-Madaniyyah.* Mullā Amīn, as his book shows, was a brilliant and learned man. In general, those who found a school, no matter how baseless, rigid and false its teachings may be, are brilliant and intelligent men. A dullard cannot found a school and gather followers around himself. The dullards, however, are influenced by those brilliant individuals and become their loyal followers.

Amīn Astarābādī claims to have discovered some truths which nobody before him had succeeded in knowing. Also, he claims a kind of Divine inspiration for himself; in the introduction to the *Fawā'id al- madaniyyah*, he says:

And you (i.e. the reader), after having gone through our book, will find in it truths untouched by any of the early or latter philosophers, legists, scholastics, and jurisprudent, and yet they are only a sample of what my Lord, the Almighty and the Supreme, has granted to me.

In this book he challenges even the philosophers and the *mutakallimūn*, as occasionally he has to discuss some issues related to philosophy and *kalām*. In the book's tenth chapter, he discusses the meaning of *nafs al-'amr*. The eleventh chapter is named by him "*Fī bayān aghlāt al-Ashā'irah wa al-Mu'tazilah fī awwal al-wajibāt*" ("On the mistakes of the Ashā'irah and the Mu'tazilah about the first obligations"). In the twelfth, he cites the mistakes of Muslim philosophers and theologians.

Amīn Astarābādī under different pretexts, tried to deny the legal authority (*ḥujjiyyah*) of three of the four well-known sources of law, that is, the *Qur'an*, *ijmā'*, and *'aql*, thus recognizing only the Sunnah as the reliable source. As to the *Qur'an*, he claimed that no one has the right to refer directly to the *Qur'an* and to interpret it.

Only the Infallible Imāms have such a right. Our duty is to refer to their *aḥādīth*. Only those parts of the *Qur'an* that have been explained in *ḥadīth* may be referred to for legal purposes; other parts whose exegesis does not exist in *ḥadīth* may not be acted upon. Also in order to deny the authenticity of the text of the *Qur'an*,

Amīn Astarābādī raised the issue of its corruption (*taḥrīf*).

As to *ijmā'*, he denied its validity, considering it an innovation (*bid'ah*) of the *sunnīs*. He also offered many arguments to deny the authority of reason. On the contrary, with respect to *aḥādīth* he went to the other extreme and claimed that all the traditions, especially those of *al-Kāfī*, *Man lā Yaḥḍuruhu al-Faqīh*, *al-Tahdhīb* and *al-Istibṣār* are of certain authenticity and legally binding. He ferociously attacked al-'Allāmah al-Ḥillī, who had classified traditions into *ṣaḥīḥ*, *muwaththaq*, *ḥasan*, and *ḍa'īf*, and occasionally insults the 'Allāmah and his followers in his book.

He categorically rejected the very principle of *ijtihād* (even in its latter sense in which the *shī'ah fuqahā'* had accepted it) and regarded it as an innovation in the faith. No one has any right to follow anyone except an infallible Imām , he claimed. He brought the entire force of his opposition to bear against reason and its authority. He claimed that all innovations involving reason - such as regarding *ijtihād* as legitimate, considering the *ẓawāhir* (apparent meanings of the Qur'anic verses) to be of binding authority, classifying *aḥādīth* into weak and strong, inquiring into the reliability of transmitters of *aḥādīth* and the like - came into vogue because the *fuqahā'* have followed the practitioners of *qiyās*, the scholastics, philosophers, and logicians to rely upon reason.

Now, if Mullā Amīn were to prove that reason is liable to error except in matters relating to objects of sense - experience or those which are derived from it (such as the concepts of mathematics), the *fuqahā'* would no longer go after *ijtihād* and reason. Accordingly, he advanced rather forceful arguments to disprove the authority of reason in matters which are not perceptual or derived from sense-experience. He is especially keen to prove that metaphysics and theology, since they are based on pure reasoning, are devoid of any value; hence the title of the twelfth chapter of *the Fawā'id al-Madaniyyah*:

On part of the errors of philosophers and

Muslim theosophist (*ḥukamā'*) in their sciences and that their cause-as we have proved earlier-is that no one who deals with the issues whose preliminaries are extra-sensible is secure from error except the Infallible Ones (the Prophet (S), Fāṭimah (A.S.), and the twelve Imāms [A.S.]).

There, he discusses some well-known problems of philosophy, such as the necessity of an intervening rest between two reciprocating straight line motions, that something which is necessarily associated with some impossibility is also impossible, the problem of precedence, and the problem of the preponderance of will.

On the whole, he is of the opinion that reason can be a guide only in the study of problems related to the natural sciences, which are based upon sense-experience, and in that of mathematics, whose concepts are derived from such experience or are closely related to it, but not in problems of theology and metaphysics. This view agrees totally with the outlook of the

European empiricists of the sixteenth century.

Incidentally, the period in which Astarābādī lived approximately coincides with that of the emergence of empiricism in Europe. It is not known whether his views were original or he had borrowed them. All that we know about him at the present is that he lived in Makkah for nearly ten years where he studied under Muḥammad Astarābādī, to whom he refers as a *faqīh*, a *mutakallim*, and philosopher. After that he had spent several years at al-Madinah. But we know nothing about how he came to adopt those views, whether he had innovated them or had borrowed them from someone else.

Amīn Astarābādī himself, and his followers as well, do not consider him as the founder of a new school called Akhbārism. Rather they consider him a revivalist who restored the way of the early *shīʿah* scholars of *ḥadīth*. They claim that their way is the same as that of the early *shīʿah* that was followed until the times of al-Shaykh al-Ṣadūq and from which the people were gradually led astray by such scholars as

Ibn Abī 'Aqīl, Ibn Junayd, al-Shaykh al-Mufīd, al-Sayyid al-Murtaḍā, and al-Shaykh al-Ṭūsī, who brought in reason and *ijtihād* to temper with Divine commands.

Shaykh Yūsuf Ibn Aḥmad al-Baḥranī (d. 1186/1772), the author of *al-Ḥadā'iq al-nāẓirah*, who was himself a moderate Akhbārī, in the tenth muqaddimah of *al-Ḥadā'iq al-Nāẓirah*, under a heading style "*Fī ḥujjiyyat al-dalīl al-'aqlī*" (On the legal validity of rational grounds), cites the following words of Sayyid Ni'mat Allah al-Jazā'irī from the latter's work al-*Anwār al-Nu'māniyyah*:

To be certain, a majority of our companions (i.e. the *shī'ah*) followed a group of our opponents, among them philosophers. Naturalists, or Ahl al-Ra'y and others, who, relying upon reason and its arguments. cast away the teachings of the prophets when they did not agree with their intellects.

In these words, which hint at excommunication, Sayyid Ni'mat Allah al-Jazā'irī considers the majority of *shīʿah* scholars - and along with them the philosophers, the naturalists, and those who follow *ra'y* and *qiyās* to be heedless of the teachings of prophets, merely on the ground that they recognize the authority of reason. By the 'majority' he means all the scholars who came after al-Shaykh al-Ṣadūq, as if until that time all *shīʿah* had been Akhbāris.

In fact Akhbāris had never existed before as a school with distinct doctrines such as those based on the denial of the authority of the *ẓawāhir* of the *Qur'an*, the denial of the authority of reason, impermissibility of the *taqlīd* of anyone except the Maʿṣūm and so on.

It is true that there were some who seldom went beyond quoting traditions in their books - even quoting them verbatim in their *fatawā*. But the fact is that the abundance of *aḥādīth* on the one hand, and the accessibility to the Imāms of the Ahl al-Bayt (A.S.) on the other, had been the major cause that the need for *ijtihād* and the need to deduce particular rules from general laws had not yet been felt.

Al-Shaykh al-Ṭūsī, in the introduction to *al-Mabsūṭ*, says: "I had heard from the 'Āmmah (i.e. the *sunnīs*) the criticism that our *fiqh* is limited because we do not practice *qiyās* and *ra'y* and is therefore also inadequate for answering all the problems.

For years I had been desirous of writing a work on legal deduction without having recourse to *qiyās* and *ra'y*, deducing in it particular rules (*Furū'*) from the fundamental general principles (*uṣūl*) that we have been taught in traditions. However, various preoccupations and hindrances prevented it." Then he adds:

My determination was weakened further by the absence of any desire on the part of this sect (i.e. the Imāmiyyah) towards it and their indifference in this regard; because they have compiled the traditions which they relate with their familiar vocabulary, to the extent that if in a problem different words to which they are not used to are employed to convey the same sense, they consider it as an odd thing.

Al-Ṭūsī makes it clear that the biggest impediment in his writing of such a book was that it was not yet customary among the *shī'ah* to practice *ijtihād* and to deduce particulars from universals.

As said before, there had not emerged any great jurist until that time who could officially practice *ijtihād* and deduce particular rules from the general principles. There had been some - such as al-Shaykh al-Ṣadūq, Ibn al-Walīd, and others - whose method was based on narration of traditions, not on a discursive study of the subject. Even if they wrote any book on *kalām*, their argument consisted mainly of traditions.

It was they whom al-Shaykh al-Ṭūsī calls '*muqallidah*' (imitators) and criticizes them. Al-Sayyid al-Murtaḍā - as quoted in the introduction to *al-Sarā'ir* by Ibn Idrīs - refers to them as *aṣḥāb al-ḥadīth min aṣḥābinā* (the 'Ahl al-Ḥadīth' from among our companions), and al-'Allāmah al-Ḥillī, in *Tahdhīb al-Uṣūl*, calls them '*al-akhbāriyyīn min aṣḥābinā*' (the 'Akhbārīs'-traditionists-from among our companions).

Perhaps it is on this account that al-Shahristānī, in *al-Milal wa al- Niḥal*, divides the Imāmiyyah into the sub sects of Mu'tazilah and Akhbāris. In the first volume of his work, he says:

When there came to be divergence in the traditions narrated from their Imāms, as time passed every group of them took its own way, and some of the Imāmiyyah became either Mu'tazilah, or Wa'īdiyyah, or Tafḍīliyyah, or Akhbāriyyah, or Mushabbihah, or Salafiyyah.

However, it is quite certain and definite that in the early era there was no school opposed to that of *ijtihād* and legal deduction amongst the *shī'ah* to have challenged the authority of the *ẓawāhir* of the *Qur'an* or the authority of reason in order to defend *ḥadīth.*

The appearance of Akhbārism, as I have said before, was a catastrophe for the scientific and intellectual life of the *shī'ah.* Many individuals came to adopt its teachings and came to look down upon reason and rationalism. They made reflection upon the *Qur'an* a taboo and, instead of making the *Qur'an* the criterion for the acceptability of *ḥadīth*, made *ḥadīth* a criterion for the *Qur'an*.

Fortunately there emerged eminent personalities among the *mujtahidūn* and *uṣūlīs* who fought the influence of the Akhbāris. Among them the names of Waḥīd Bihbihānī and Shaykh Murtaḍā al-Anṣārī - may God elevate their station - stand high. To describe in detail the services of these two personages is beyond the scope of the present study.

By the way, it should not remain unsaid that the struggle against Akhbārism was a difficult and complex matter because its teachings took a deceptive and self-righteous stance which misled the public. It was for this reason that they rapidly gained influence and popularity after Amīn Astarābādī ...

As is known, there broke out severe and bloody conflict towards the end of the second/eighth century and the beginning of the third/ninth between the Ahl al-Ḥadīth wa al-Sunnah, who resemble the *shī'ah* Akhbāris, and the Mu'tazilah, who believe in the role of reason and the validity of rational arguments. Al-Ma'mūn (r. 198-218/813- 833), who was personally a man of learning, supported the Mu'tazilah and backed them in the controversy about the creation of the *Qur'an.*

He sent out a circular declaring those who denied the creature-hood of the *Qur'an* as heretics, who had no right to be judges and preside over the courts of law nor was their testimony to be accepted in the courts. As a result the Mu'tazilah attained great power during al-Ma'mūn's reign. More philosophical works than at any other time were translated into Arabic during al-Ma'mūn's reign and rationalism became prevalent when al-Mutawakkil (r. 232-247/846-861) came to power, he reversed the tide by throwing the weight of his support behind the Ahl al-Ḥadīth. The Mu'tazilah were proscribed and the publication of philosophy was banned. Al-Mas'ūdī, in *Murūj al-Dhahab*, writes:

> When the caliphate fell to al-Mutawakkil, he ordered the people to abstain from discussion and debate and whatever they were used to in the days of al-Mu'taṣim and al-Wāthiq. He directed them to adopt compliance and imitation.

Al-Mutawakkil's support for the Ahl al-Ḥadīth wa al-Sunnah - who like the *shī'ah* Akhbāris had a deceptively self-righteous stance, spoke untiringly of submission and devotion and persistently chanted the phrase *qāla Rasūl Allah* ('so said the Apostle of Allah') - had an extraordinary effect on the people, to whom it appeared to be a defence of the Prophet. For this reason, al-Mutawakkil, despite his tyranny and debauchery, came to assume saintly image in the popular mind.

The Mu'tazilah could never recover from that blow. And we, the *shī'ah*, should thank God that there arose no Mutawakkil in the era of the emergence of the *shī'ah* Akhbāris, who were a hundred times more obscurantists and formalistic than the Ahl al-Ḥadīth wa al-Sunnah, in their defence.

However, we should note the point that even though the Akhbārī onslaught was defeated through the courageous resistance of a number of the followers of the school of *ijtihād*, but the Akhbārī thinking was not completely destroyed.

Whenever the champions of *ijtihād* have made any headway and wherever they have put their feet, Akhbārī thinking had to recede and disappear. But Akhbārī obscurantism still rules in those places where they were not able to reach.

How often we come across mujtahids who do *ijtihād* with an Akhbārī brain. Many of the kind of things which are published in the name of the 'teachings of the Ahl al-Bayt' and come to the market, but which strike dagger into the back of the Ahl al-Bayt of the Prophet (S), are no more than the remnants of the thought of Mullā Muḥammad Amīn Astarābādī.

Bibliography

The Holy *Qur'an*.

Aḥmad Ḥanbal, *Musnad*,(Beirut: Mu'assasah al-Risālah , 1421 A.H.).

Ḥussain Nūrī al-Ṭabrisī, *Mustadrak al-Wasā'il wa Mustanbaṭ al-Masā'il*, (Beirut: Mu'assasah Āl al-Bayt li Iḥyā' al-Turāth, 1408 A.H.).

Index

A

Abān Ibn Taghlib, 8
Abū Ḥāmid Muḥammad al-Ghazālī, 22
Abū Ḥanīfah, 15, 16, 17, 22
Adillah, 13, 36, 37
Africa, 41
Ahl al-Bayt, 8, 9, 35, 37, 40, 51, 58
Ahl al-Ḥadīth, 18, 19, 34, 35, 36, 37, 39, 56, 57, 58
Ahl al-Ra'y, 18, 50
Ahl al-Sunnah, 16, 17
Aḥmad Ibn Ḥanbal, 17
Akhbāriyyah, 54
al-'amal bi al-ra'y, 13, 15
'Alawīd, 37
al-Azhar, 25
al-Fawā'id al- Madaniyyah,43, 47,44
al-Ghazālī, 32
al-Ḥadā'iq al-Nāẓirah, 50
al-ḥusn wa al-qubḥ al-'aqliyyah, 18, 34, 37
al-Imām al-Bāqir, 8
al-Imām al-Ṣādiq, 9
al-Inṣāf fī Bayān Sabab al-Ikhtilāf, 24
al-Istibṣār, 46
al-Kāfī, 35, 46
al-Khiṭaṭ, 23
'Allāmah Shaykh Maḥmūd Shaltūt, 25
Al-Ma'mūn, 56
al-Mabsūṭ, 52

al-Malik al-Ẓāhir, 23
Al-Mas'ūdī, 57
al-Milal wa al- Niḥal, 54
al-Miqfrīzī, 23
al-mujtahid al-muṭlaq, 21
al-Mustaṣfā, 32
al-Mu'taṣim, 57
al-Mutawakkil, 56, 57
al-Sarā'ir, 53
al-Shāfi'ī, 15, 17
al-Shaykh al-Ṣadūq, 49, 51, 53
al-Shaykh al-Ṭūsī, 32, 50, 53
al-Tahdhīb, 46
al-Wāthiq, 57
Amīn Astarābādī, 43, 44, 45, 46, 47, 49, 55, 58
'āmm, 14
Anwār al-Nu'māniyyah, 50
Ashā'irah, 19, 34, 35, 37, 45
Āyatullāh, al-'Allāmah al-Ḥillī, 8

D

ḍa'īf, 46
Dā'irat al-Ma'ārif, 24
Dāwūd Ibn 'Alī al-Ẓāhirī al-Iṣfahānī, 17

E

Egypt, 23
exercising of one's opinion or judgement, 13
express text (*naṣṣ*), 15

F

faqāhah, 14
faqīh, 14, 17, 21, 33, 49
Farīd al-Wajdī, 24
Fāṭimah, 48
fatwā, 8, 9, 21, 22, 25

H

ḥalāl, 19, 36
Ḥanafī, 20, 21, 23
Ḥanbalī, 20, 23, 41, 43
ḥarām, 19, 36
ḥasan, 23, 46
Ḥijāz, 16
ḥujjah, 16

I

Ibn Abī 'Aqīl, 50
Ibn al-Ṣabbāgh, 22

Ibn al-Walīd, 53
Ibn Idrīs, 53
Ibn Khaldūn, 42
Ibn Khallekān, 17
iftā', 8
ijmā', 12, 13, 15, 36, 45, 46
Ijtihād, 7, 22
'ilm al-uṣūl, 12
Imām al-Ḥaramayn al-Juwaynī, 22
Imāms, 8, 9, 16, 22, 23, 24, 25, 35, 40, 45, 48, 51, 54
Islamic law, 13
'Irāqī school, 17
Islamic legislation, 13
istiḥsān, 15

J

jabr (fatalism), 37
Ja'farī school, 25
jurisprudence, 2, 12, 22, 24, 26, 36, 38, 39, 41

K

kalām, 16, 18, 26, 29, 34, 45, 53
khāṣṣ, 14

L

legal authority (*ḥujjiyyah*), 45

M

Ma'ṣūm, 51
Madinah, 9, 17, 49
Maghrib, 41
Makkah, 49
Mālik Ibn Anas, 17
Mālikī, 20, 23
Man lā Yaḥḍuruhu al-Faqīh, 46
mansūkh, 14
mashhūr, 15
Mu'ādh, 11
mubayyan, 14
muftī, 25
muḥaddith, 17
Muḥammad, 21, 22, 23, 49, 58
Muḥammad Ibn Jarīr al-Ṭabarī, 21, 23
muḥkam, 14
mujmal, 14
mujtahid, 7, 8, 22
mujtahidūn, 20, 55
mukhaṭṭi'ah, 26
muqallidah, 53

Murūj al-Dhahab, 57
muṣawwibah, 26
Mushabbihah, 54
mustafīḍ, 15
mutakallim, 49
mutakallimūn, 44
mutashābih, 14
Mu'tazilah, 18, 19, 34, 35, 37, 45, 54, 56, 57
muwaththaq, 46

N

nafs al-'amr, 45
nāsikh, 14

P

particular rules, 51, 53
particular rules (*Furū'*), 52
Prophet(S), IX, 7, 11, 12, 14, 15, 27, 31, 32, 33, 48, 57, 58

Q

qiyās, 13, 14, 16, 17, 18, 27, 31, 32, 33, 34, 35, 36, 37, 38, 39, 40, 47, 51, 52
Qur'an, 13, 14, 45, 51, 54, 55, 56

R

ra'y, 18, 19, 27, 31, 32, 33, 34, 35, 36, 37, 38, 39, 40, 51, 52

S

ṣaḥīḥ, 46
ṣawāb, 26
Sayyid al-Murtaḍā, 50, 53
Sayyid Ni'mat Allah al-Jazā'irī, 50, 51
Shāfi'ī, 15, 20, 21, 23
Shāh Walī Allah Dihlawī, 24
Shahristānī, 54
sha'n al-nuzūl, 14
Sharī'ah, 13, 15, 18, 27, 32, 33, 35, 36, 38
Shaykh Abū Ja'far al-Ṭūsī, 31
Shaykh al-Mufīd, 50
Shaykh Murtaḍā al-Anṣārī, 55
Shaykh Yūsuf Ibn Aḥmad al-Baḥranī, 50
shī'ah, 7, 8, 9, 26, 27, 28, 29, 31, 33, 34, 35, 36, 37, 38, 40, 43, 46, 49, 50, 51, 53, 54, 56, 57

Shīʿism, 8
Sufyān al-Thawrī, 23
Sunnī, 7
Sunnī fuqahā', 8, 9, 15, 26, 27

T

ta'awwul, 15
Tafḍīliyyah, 54
Tahdhīb al-Uṣūl, 34, 53
taḥrīf, 46
takhṭi'ah, 26, 29, 31
taqlīd, 2, 51
tashbīh (anthropomorphism), 38
taṣwīb, 26, 27, 28, 29, 31
tawḥīd, 37

U

'Uddat al-Uṣūl, 31
Umayyad, 37
'Unwān al-Baṣrī, 9
uṣūlīs, 55

W

Waḥīd Bihbihānī, 55
Waʿīdiyyah, 54

Z

Ẓāhirī, 17, 20, 23, 36, 41, 43

www.ingramcontent.com/pod-product-compliance
Lightning Source LLC
Chambersburg PA
CBHW021450080526
44588CB00009B/786